PINOCCHIO
The Cricket's Tale

Leeds Trinity University

LIBRARY

**This book is due for return on or before
the last date stamped below**

PINOCCHIO
The Cricket's Tale

Retold by Sara Stanley

Illustrated by Nigel Potter

Network**Educational**Press Ltd

*To Ellen, Susie, Jessica, Millie, Imogen, Esmé, Thomas, Jack, Eleanor and Lucy
who always listen to their crickets — and to my three who don't!*

S.S.

*To Madeline and Joe, for putting up with me being around; Holly and Hannah
for putting up with me not being around; and my Father whom I would very
much like to have around.*

N.P.

Published by Network Educational Press Ltd
PO Box 635
Stafford
ST16 1BF

First published 2004
Text © Sara Stanley 2004
Illustrations © Nigel Potter 2004
ISBN 1 85539 164 3

Editor: Debbie Pullinger
Art director: Chris Fraser

Printed in Great Britain by Technographic, Colchester, Essex

Some people believe that from the minute
they are born, something or someone special
watches over them, helping them to choose
between right and wrong.

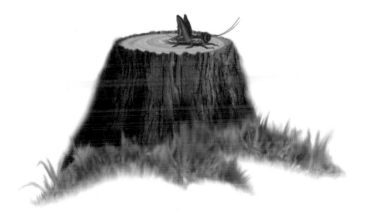

That's me! Some people call me a conscience,
but I prefer to be called a friend.

I live in the cottage of an old carpenter called Geppetto, which is where my story begins. Geppetto had been given a fine piece of wood, and he decided to carve it into a puppet. But what Geppetto did not know was that this was no ordinary piece of wood.

When Geppetto had finished his work, the little wooden puppet sat up, blinked the sawdust from his eyes – and stuck out his tongue. He was alive!

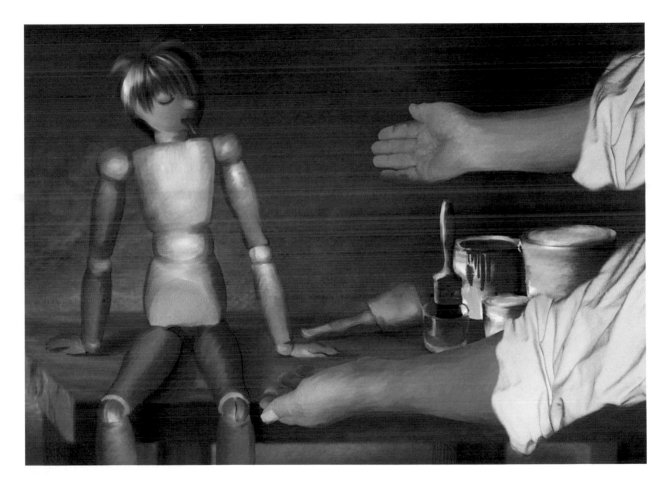

The old man was overjoyed to have a son at last, and named him Pinocchio.

It soon became clear that Pinocchio was not only full of life – but also full of mischief. He did not want to obey his father, Geppetto, and he certainly did not want to go to school.

From my spot on the wall, I watched Pinocchio being rude and silly. I felt sorry for him because he knew he was different – trapped, as he was, in his hard, wooden body.

I explained to Pinocchio that it would be better for him if he was good – that children have to obey grown-ups and go to school. But he did not want to listen to the words I put inside his head, and my tiny voice was silenced by the thud of a mallet.

When Pinocchio saw what he had done, the tears rolled down his wooden face and he begged me to help him learn to be a real boy. He bandaged my broken wing and promised he would go to school.

Next morning we set off. On the way to the school house, we saw a sign for a puppet theatre. Forgetting his promise and ignoring my voice in his ear, Pinocchio ran off to see the show.

Inside the theatre Pinocchio was dazzled by the lights and the music. He wanted to be part of the show and leaped up onto the stage. The audience loved the little puppet who danced without strings, and they threw him their gold.

Afterwards Pinocchio ran home, eager to give the money to his poor old father.

On the road, he ran into a wily fox and a mean old cat. Seeing the gold, they planned to trick Pinocchio. "Over by the river is the field of miracles," they told him. "Go and plant your coins there. When you return the next morning, you will have a beautiful money tree."

D elighted by their promises of money and happiness, Pinocchio did as the cunning creatures suggested. Nothing I said could change his mind.

When Pinocchio got back to the cottage, Geppetto demanded to know where he had been. "I was at school," Pinocchio said. No sooner had the words left his mouth, than his nose started to grow.

"But why are you so late?" asked Geppetto. "I stayed on for extra lessons," Pinocchio replied. With each question his father asked, Pinocchio told another lie. And with each lie he told, his nose grew longer and longer.

"Tell the truth, Pinocchio!" I shouted, from the far end of his nose. Pinocchio was filled with shame. He promised to be honest – and his nose shrank back to its usual size.

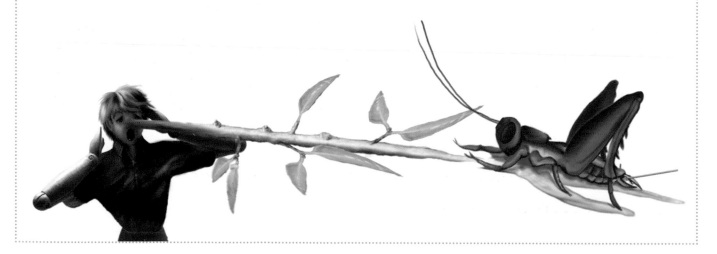

As he lay in bed, Pinocchio thought of his money tree and the branches laden with golden coins. If only he could bring home some of the gold, then his father might forgive him. "Go to sleep," I whispered, but he slipped away into the night.

Pinocchio searched the field for his tree, but found only a hole and two sets of paw prints. He felt too foolish and embarrassed to return home.

ext morning, a group of boys wandered past. They said they were going to Playland – a place where there were no grown-ups and no rules. Everything was free and boys could play all day. "Come with us!" they shouted.

In Playland, Pinocchio and the boys were free to have fun – bad fun! Pinocchio soon forgot about Geppetto and me, and thought he could be lazy and selfish for ever.

Little did he know what punishment lay ahead. The bad life seemed just fine, until the day he noticed he had a tail and furry ears … and felt soft grey fur sprouting all over his body. He was changing …

… into a donkey!

Poor Pinocchio was dragged away to a farm where his cruel master made him work from dawn to dusk. When I heard his sad cry I knew this was my friend. I told him how his father loved him and missed him badly. My words made his heart and body ache until he could no longer walk or stand.

Now that he was no use to his owner, Pinocchio the donkey was cast into the sea to drown.

S oon the salty sea water washed away his donkey skin and the little wooden puppet began to swim home.

We were nearing the shore when suddenly there was a dreadful roar and a gush of water.

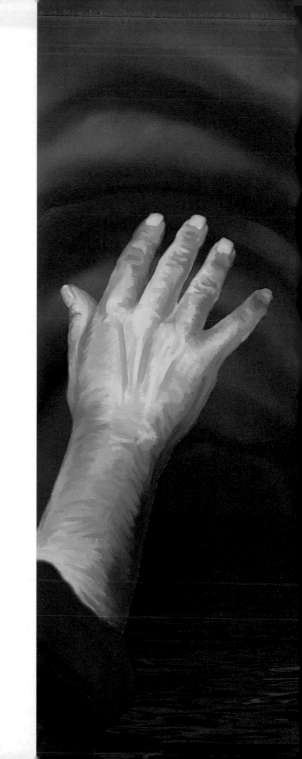

As our eyes adjusted to the darkness inside the whale's belly, we peered through the seaweedy gloom and saw... Geppetto. Pinocchio rushed into his father's arms.

Geppetto told his son how he had searched for him over land and sea until, one stormy night, he was swept into the ocean and swallowed by the whale. Pinocchio saw how weak and ill his father was, and made a plan for our escape. He lit a fire and waited.

A- A- A- Tissshoooooo!

We were wafted out to freedom on the whale's smoky sneeze.

On the long journey home, Pinocchio looked after his father.

In every town where we stayed, he worked hard to get money for food and medicine. Little by little, Geppetto regained his strength.

inally we arrived at Geppetto's cottage, where
Pinocchio fell into bed, exhausted.

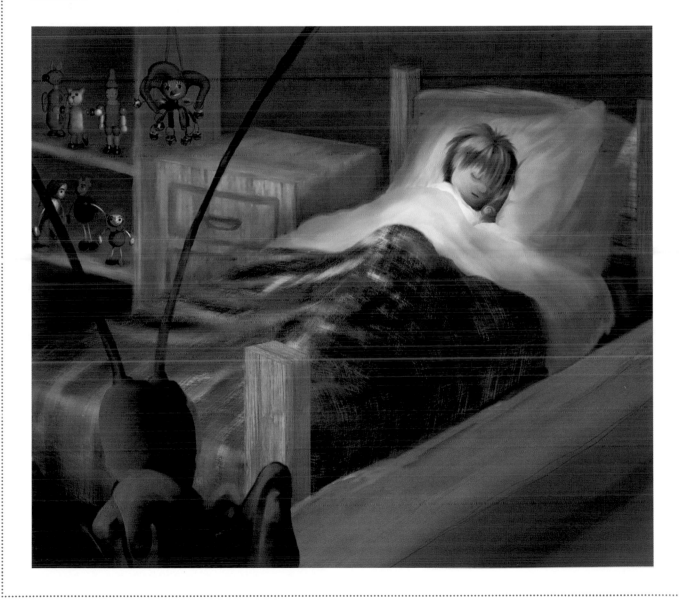

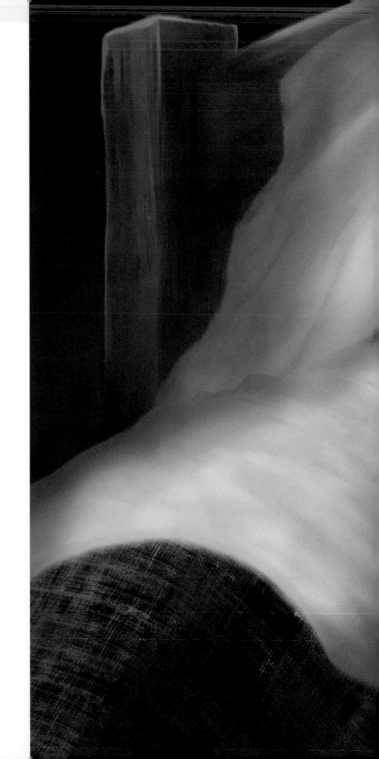

And now, as I watch Pinocchio sleeping peacefully, a gentle warmth seeps into his body. I whisper in his ear – which is no longer a wooden ear – secret words you may have heard at your birth but don't remember. Words that help you make the best choices in life.

Even in his sleep, Pinocchio now knows what it means to be real.

The End